Poetic Grenade

also by Ngozi Olivia Osuoha

The Transformation Train
Letter to My Unborn
Sensation
Fruits from the Poetry Planet
Tropical Escape (co-author)

Poetic Grenade

by
Ngozi Olivia Osuoha

Poetic Justice Books & Arts
Port Saint Lucie, Florida

©2019 Ngozi Olivia Osuhua

book design and layout: SpiNDec, Port Saint Lucie, FL
cover image: *Splash*, ©2018 Kris Haggblom

All rights reserved.

No part of this book may be used or reproduced in any manner whatsoever without written permission except in the case of brief quotations embodied in critical articles and reviews. Members of educational institutions and organizations wishing to photocopy any of the work for classroom use, or authors, artists and publishers who would like to obtain permission for any material in the work, should contact the publisher.

Published by Poetic Justice Books
Port Saint Lucie, Florida
www.poeticjusticebooks.com

ISBN: 978-1-950433-12-4

FIRST EDITION
10 9 8 7 6 5 4 3 2 1

DEDICATION

This poetry book is dedicated to the administrators and members of Poetry Planet, Planet For The Budding Poets, World Peace And Harmony Association (Literature Lovers' Association), Asian Literary Society and POEMarium (Philippines and India).

table of contents

A World of Butterflies 3
Trouble 4
Fortune 5
Time 6
Dream 7
Fragrance 8
Memory 9
Innocence 10
First Love 11
Relief 12
Peace 13
Festival of Lights 14
Dark World 15
Sandcastle 16
Happiness 17
Legacy 18
My Child 19
That Pain 20
Festival of Light 21
Social Media 22
My Candle 23
Future 24
We Are One 25
Spirituality 26
Change 27
Traumatized 28
Dear Moon 29
Believe in Yourself 30
Second Chance 31
Purple Couple 32
Wondrous Winter 33
Look at the Sky 34
I Will Survive 35
Dear Cliff 36
Village Life 37
Dear Santa 38
Let Go 39
Careless Whisper 40
Dreams 41
Christmas - Inner Joy of Light and Peace 42
Special Children 43

Stardust	44
Here Comes My Hero	45
Legacies	46
My Footprints	48
My Only Wish	49
Art	50
Unmeltable	51
Wish	52
Prejudice	53
Lost	54
The Reading Ghost	55
Bandit	56
Banditry	57
Cocoon	58
My Shield	59
Vision	60
Locomotive	62
Heavy Duty	63
Confusion	65
Troubled	66
The Guardian Dragon	67
The Park	68
Negligence	69
Neglected	70
Mr. Bean	72
Tear the Mask	73
Hurricane	75
Conclusion	76
Friendship	78
We Are Friends	79
The Venom of a Poet	81
My Ink	83
Surrounded	85
Delighted in You	86
Camouflage	88
Scandals	89
Falsehood	90
If You See Our Soldiers	92
Camouflage	94
Virgin Santa	96
When Spring Comes	97
about the author	99

Poetic Grenade

A World of Butterflies

This is our world
We live it to the fullest
Spread our wings to the highest
Enjoy the limitless bounds
And reach the boundless limit.

Trouble

Life is a hurdle
More than a triple jump
It gives double for a trouble
Life is also a game
It can bring shame
It can as well
bring fame.

Fortune

Fortune yields green gold
Enlivening the seeker
eternally in peace
That he may long no more
But when fortunes get lost
Life seems unbearable.

Time

Time and tide rock and roll
Stage and page slide and hide
Events and occasions come and go
Seasons bear reasons in unison
Born, live, die, we all
Change is not strange.

Dream

Pregnant with this child
Restless with this dream
Sleepless nights and lonely days
Troubled noons with empty stomach
Hungry morning, thirsty and hopeless
Yet this dream keeps coming and pushing.

No appetite for the best dish
No freedom to mingle among
Because this dream is unborn.

Whether in light or in darkness
Whether in rich or in poor
Wherever, however, whenever, whatever,
I must put to birth my dreams
Because I know dreams come true.

Fragrance

My fragrance
You are my aura
And my power,
When I look at you
I see myself through
The fragrance you exude
Is what I inhale,
You exhibit pride and valour
That, makes me move in wonder,
Just the audacity of hope
That wraps me in elegance
I dare not judge your flow
Because your frequency turns me on,
I never question your charisma
For your confidence rides my glory,
This fragrance is naturally resourceful
The force radiates like the sun's rays
And gets me engrossed
In the cravings and yearnings of my heart
Where my soul finds a zealous love
In your spirit.

Memory

Though it fades with time and age
I thank God for such a recorder in our head
We grow from birth and encounter many things
Good, bad, fair, evil, great, small
We love some, others we hate
We need some, others we discard
We accept some and reject others
Life plays us like a guitar
And we dance to the music
But whatever happens, there are times we sit back and ponder
Trying to recall even if not chronologically
Tears, be they joyful or sorrowful
Times, past, present or future
We wish, regret, repent and hope
These memories fold or wrap up our activities on earth

Innocence

She was a poor girl
Beautiful, respectful and wonderful
She had dreams, hopes and aspirations
But was too tender to understand life was a prankster.

They enticed and wooed her deeply
They fought hard to have her
They went extra miles to bring her down
But she thought they were real
So, she chose one,
Unfortunately, the wrong one.

Mesmerized, battered and violated
Here she is with a child out of wedlock,
The trickster of life robbed her of her innocence.

Confused, betrayed and deceived
Nothing makes sense anymore.

First Love

Like a rose it blossoms
reddish, like blood
Flowing deep and wide
Longing to be ever close
Real, though immature
Committed, even from afar
Dedicated, despite lack.

Like a champion, he wins
Like a hero, he rules
Like a friend, always near
Reasonable over nonsense
Understanding the hard issues
Until all of a sudden
an eye-opener
there it ends with a well of lessons.

Relief

Just chatted with a friend
And the relief is unimaginable,
Good, for today.

Peace

We cannot actually tell
The true value of peace
Until we finally lose it.

Festival of Lights

We cannot afford to live in the dark
For we were born to do exploits
This world is ours to rebuild
Come, let's begin the festival of lights.

Dark World

To a little girl
Growing up in the hood
Everything is dark
Even the birds in the air
The little light I see
Is never enough for the world.

Sandcastle

I will build mum a castle
And a skyscraper
I will build dad an empire
And a palace
I will build my brothers a mansion
And my sisters a paradise
Let them all be happy.

I will not let them suffer
I will provide everything for them
So they experience heaven before heaven.

I will not build them a sandcastle
Because it is not real,
Rains and winds would scatter them
Floods swipe and sweep them away.

No, I will not build a sandcastle.

Happiness

In a world of wars and trouble
Where lives are never safe
In a world of insanity
Where madness is the king
In a world of evil
Where killing, murder and injustice reign
How can one define happiness?

Soaked land with blood
Blood of the poor and innocent,
Wasted daily here and there
A world so full of hate, anger and terrorism
Who dares talk of happiness?

Happiness eludes us
Our loved ones die unnecessarily
Leaving young widows, pregnant wives, aged parents
Some unborn and fatherless
Who in this world is really happy?

Legacy

Life is vanity
When based on materialism
No matter our wealth
Our connections and acquisitions
They all end when we are gone.

But honesty, loyalty and integrity
Diligence, goodwill and good name
These are our legacies, they are everlasting.

Our actions are words on marble
The histories we make
The lives we save, the change we create
All these legacies outlive us.

Our soul is not for the grave.

My Child

Dear child
Listen to me
I am your mother,
Please heed to my instructions
For life to be well with you.

I have seen many things in life
Peace, trouble, love, hate and discrimination
Betrayal, gossip, ridicule,
Scandal and slandering
Please listen attentively.

Life is a field of all events
Be ready to see all,
Prepare for the worst while you hope for the best,
Friends kill, brothers sell
Dreams die, hopes dwindle
Just remember that I told you before time.

But cheer up, give your all
The lord be with you.

Be strong all the time
Guard and guide yourself always,
Never look down on anyone
Because angels don't always wear white
Be fair and friendly in all your doings.

That Pain

Hmm, it is a very long story
But let me start from somewhere
How my joy was thwarted
How my hope was dashed
How my happiness was cut short
How my pain turned my gain.

When you expected much
And believed really
When you hoped high
And prayed so fervent,
When you waited long
And needed patiently,
When you deserved honour
But were clothed with shame,
That pain, O that pain
The very pain that became so much a gain.

The shock that taught me shield
The lies that taught me truth
The gossip that taught me hate
The black tongue that taught me the horrors of man.

Festival of Light

I light my candle
To light the world,
Let there be light
To banish this darkness
For us to bear light
And live beyond darkness.

Social Media

Social media
The route to fame
The place of character and actors
The abode of pretenders and liars.

A channel that brews fakery
A show of pride, arrogance and rudeness
A shameless zone and mannerless territory
Social media, an enemy of godliness.

The opposite of discipline and censorship
A wave and storm of all kinds of waywardness,
A path of doom, deceit and betrayal
Social media and world of uncertainties.

However social media hope of civilization
The track of all news and communication
A lift in mankind and humanity.

My Candle

I bear a candle
To light the world
I will not let it go out
No matter the wind.

I know the breeze
Soothing, or ravaging and harsh
I know the hurricane
Destructive, overwhelming and cruel
But I will not allow my candle to be quenched

This candle is the hope of many
It is the joy of the unborn
A light to those in darkness
A great lead way to paths unknown
I dare not let it dwindle.

Future

The future is a mystery
No one knows it,
It is deep
No one fathoms it,
It is a secret
No one tells it,
But people live for it.

The future is a payer
Everyone, according to their coin,
The future is a god
Very strange, it can change
The range and duration
No one vows about it.

The future is a mystery
We can make it a history,
If we hate to be in misery
Let us work from the nursery.

We Are One

You are my true love
Hold me and hold on for me
Be with me through thick and thin
Let us conquer the world for each other
And enjoy it together
We are one; heart, body and soul.

Spirituality

The world is a camouflage
It represents the spiritual realm,
For everything must first happen there
Before we witness it here.

The spiritual world is the true world
For we are imperfect beings here
Knowing little or nothing.

When we move close to the creator
We have a glimpse,
When we deviate, we fall out
Then, the negative spirit may take control.

Spirituality is the opposite of physicality
Both are also parallel
Fighting for and or against each other.

Change

Born into a world of changes
Where nothing is truly by chance
We struggle through everything
And hustle forever until we are gone.
All, we all change with time.

From birth to death is change
Living, growing, dying and all
Nothing is ever permanent.
Decisions, love, hate
Dreams, goals, aspirations
Visions, pursuits and all
All, they all change with time.

Seasons, time, tide and waves
Storms, mountains and valleys
Processes, procedures, and findings
Conclusions, answers and reasons
All, they all, we all keep changing.

Traumatized

Daily, I weep for my land
All night I wet my bed with tears,
I wail for my motherland
I cry as I helplessly watch my fatherland get ruined,
I am traumatized, my strength fails me,
I pray I hope not in vain.

Dear Moon

Half or full
I love your pull
You are so cool
And white like wool
Up in the cloud
Silent but loud
A light at night
For the crowd so proud
You chase the dark
When the dog can't bark.

Dear moon
Tales by moonlight
And honeymoon
Boom at full moon.

Believe in Yourself

Dear friend
Believe in yourself,
Never let the world weigh you down.

Forget the thunder and lightning
Look away from the deceits
Of storms and waves.

Find your strength and pursue your greatness
Discover your talents and rule the world,
Dig out your ore and refine it
You will be more than gold.

Life is never fair, even to angels
So, fear not the struggle,
Life is crooked even to the rugged
So, keep up the fight,
Nothing ever comes easy.

The world will reject you even when you win
The world will reject you even when you are a king,
But keep the faith, light the candle, ignite your passion
Insist, for only then the world will give way.

Second Chance

Life is a circle of pain
It creates ripples too,
Life is a cycle
It bends and breaks,
That way we are fixed.

When you encounter troubles
Double your strength,
When you face challenges
Triple your iron
That way, you sail through the storm.

Until death, do not give up
Once beaten, twice shy
But once bitten, thrice fly
That, I say to you.

Our destiny has several links
Until they are linked together, we may keep tossing
So, stay put, there is a second chance.

Suicide is never the best option,
Hang in there, the future is a mystery
You can conquer the mastery.

Purple Couple

I humbly offer you this rose
As a token of my love and submission,
It is my willingness to be with you forever
Please accept it wholeheartedly
And let our union be sealed
That pure love may greenly blossom a purple couple

Wondrous Winter

O wondrous winter
You are beautiful and gorgeous
But you make me lonely,
You dry my palms
And freeze me in bed,
Keep me longer in sleep
I hope you care for me,
Try to be gentle
For you are a wonder.

Look at the Sky

Look at the sky
You will see my star
Shining upon the earth
To light the world.

Look at the sky
You will see the galaxy
A cluster of stars
I am there with the angels
Lighting the world.

Shining, glowing, glittering
Dazzling, illuminating, twinkling
Crystal, brave, bold, golden
Look, darkness trembles.

I Will Survive

Life is not fair, so we strive
For we live the way we drive
Not because we cannot thrive
Hence to challenges I echo
I will survive.

Dear Cliff

Hold your peace
And watch life play its game
You are heavier than death
And livelier than life,
Fear not, black warrior
Never tremble, mama's hero
You are more than gold.

The pendulum shall rest
For the weight it bears is real
Real, strong and enough
It shall steady the earth,
Peace, be still
Dear Cliff, be still.

Village Life

Village life, so beautiful and unique
Born in the village, in my hometown
Bred there also, grew up with my parents,
Worked in the farm, fetched firewood
Went to the streams, fetched palm fruits too
Had barns of yam, and poultry
We worked hard for daily bread,
Dad was the teacher, mum was too
The farm we cultivated their school

Played with friends and peers
Went to church, mornings and evenings
Sent on errands, danced around with mates
Village life, a teacher, a breeder.

So much lessons for life
So much experience for a next generation
The village, a place of abundant knowledge

Growing with grandparents and elders
You learn mysteries and histories
They help shape, mould and pattern your lifestyle
Then you walk with an edge of wisdom.

Dear Santa

Dear Santa, my friend
Saint Nicholas, the favourite saint of children
The season is here
Christmas is near,
Please get us the gifts
Let our hearts be merry
We wait and pray and hope
We cannot wait any longer
Please where are the gifts

Christmas is in the air
Red, green, yellow everywhere
Jesus is born, born our saviour
Gift us Santa to celebrate our salvation.

Let Go

Understanding the world is a major work
It takes more than knowledge,
Wisdom is highly involved
And patience seriously needed,
When you come to a crossroads
And life seems terrific
Sit down, breathe and relax.

Ponder, wonder and meditate
Pray, doubt and consider
Think deep and long
Learn, relearn, unlearn
For only then you can puncture facts.

Let go of the fears, wants and needs
Let go of the traumas, dramas and dilemmas
Let go of the confusions and commotions
But never let go of your dreams.

Your visions, lane, track and path
Your coat and coast are necessary
Never let go of things that matter most.

Persist, resist, insist
Desist, time fixes all.

Careless Whisper

My lover is awesome
He is such a handsome eagle
I hear his beagle
When he blows his trumpet
I fall like his pet.

Gentle is his whisper
But distinct like a whistle,
I love his flute
I cannot keep mute,
No careless whisper
Such a holy lord.

Dreams

Here are my concrete dreams
The future I earnestly pray for
To have a unique family
One filled with outstanding children
They would not just bring me pleasure
But heal the world at large.

Christmas - Inner Joy of Light and Peace

Christmas, herald of good news
Please bring us peace and joy,
For the world is cruel and heartless
And we have been in tears for long.

Special Children

Children are gifts from God
They bring immense pleasure
Spending time with them heals
Playing with them gives them joy
Teaching them is necessary,
They are the future we seek.

Children are wonderful, they all are gifted
No matter what, how and when.

However, circumstances fluctuate
And so does life, they can come in different forms
Special children can perform wonders
They excel too in their fields like others,
Training and raising them is tedious though
But we cannot dare to get rid of them
Because they never chose to be that special.

Love, care, raise and support special children
Together, we all can change the world,
Take Paralympics for example.

Stardust

You make me a spirit
You wake my spirit
As if I am dead,
When I am dead
You awaken my soul
And put me in control
You are like the star
You shine my path
And push my darkness
You enlighten my world
And sharpen my sword,
You brighten my night
And elongate my day,
Pure stardust from heaven
Ejecting and emitting crystals of hope.

Here Comes My Hero

Look, here comes the hero
The prince of the ride
The king of the road
Give way, give way for him.

Lo, here comes the hero
The lion of the jungle
The giant of the competition
Make way, make way for him.

Lo, he rides
Speeding like the light
Flying like the kite
Cheering the firmament
Winning the fight,
O give way, make way for him.

This little tier is killing it
This future leader leading it
He is gorgeous and glorious
Excited and enthusiastic
Warm, brave, and prosperous.

The green smile on his young face
The courageous spirit of his strength
No, this warrior is not a child.

Legacies

I am aware of it
Right from when I was growing up
I knew I would not just live
The burden is in me
There is a mandate
One to be lived, loved and nurtured.

This life is not supposed to end here
I must live it so that when I leave it
Others may live it.

My dream is so loud
Despite the tiny voice in me
It burns like fire
Fighting to be born,
It struggles and aches my heart
Flogging my body,
It just would not let me be.

This legacy is not of money
Not of material possession
Not of perishable goods and wealth,
Not tangible ones
But intangible footprints
The ones that lead to worlds beyond.

On the marble, I inscribe them
As a way of life, I live them
As words I speak them

As prayers, I pray them
Interceding, fighting, encouraging
Aiding no matter how weak and little,
For I know, when I am gone
These legacies would be echoing my name.

My Footprints

I love these footprints
I will never let them be wiped
Consciously and unconsciously, I walk and work
Taking the path of patience and endurance
Persevering and pressing forward
Fighting to let my candle burn
That my light may shine in this dark world.

I will not allow these rains to sweep away my footprints
Because these footsteps are seldom to come by
Passing through thick and thin
Under the sun and in the rain
Forbearing hardships and pain
Longing and striving towards that perfect goal,
These legacies are my footmarks.

Someday, I will be gone
And someone will remember how I laboured
They will hold on to live on and to fight on
Because there will be a mirror
For them to reflect who they are.

This bargain is not mine
It is transferable to generations unborn
I dare not break it on the way
For many would be led astray.

My Only Wish

This is my only wish
To see the world become good again.

To see children live, play and study
To see them loved and cared for by their parents
I want mothers to give birth peacefully and in good health,
I wish this could come true.

I wish that there will be no more wars, no more violence,
   killings and fighting
I just wish racism, terrorism and nepotism would all
   fade away.

I really wish politics and politicians would be humane
   enough to be fair
Fair to their societies, masses and mankind,
I just wish we all would be humans again.

I wish families would be more real
True, closer, livelier and lovelier
I just wish we would never again die.

I wish no more bombs and missiles
No more religious wars and jungle justice,
I just wish this world would be forever in order

This is my only wish
To see the world become good.

Art

This is art
I love it well
The sky, river
The blue sea
The cloud
The boat and voyage.

I love the white clouds
This painting is great
The scrubs of art
Like branches of trees.

A canvas of nature
Luring gazes of peace,
Trying hard to tell
To tell the beauty of art.

Pieces of art
A mosaic and light collage
Fading into the earth
Yet deeply announcing beauty.

Unmeltable

I am a boat
Built with paper
To sail in this artistic sea,
I fear no waters
And waves do not scare me.

I forge ahead
Ahead, in my direction
I trend like the current
The splashes, the storms
I roll and row.

Do not underrate me
Never underestimate me
This little boat you see
Made of paper is titanic
Let not my body deceive you.

I sail like a captain
Meandering the tempest
I sail on my voyage
Heading for discovery.

The winds blow me
The tides hit me
The waves cheer me
The tempest, the storm
Still, ahead I race
Like a mermaid I swim
At worst, I anchor
I am unmeltable.

Wish

If wishes were all granted
Maybe we would all be gone,
Some would be slaves
Others masters, even to the lowest.

If all wishes were granted
Maybe one person would rule the world,
Maybe we all would be ghosts.

We might have been rats
Dogs, pigeons or vultures
If wishes were all granted
We would be crazy.

I would wake up and order a kill
You would wake up and have your spoil
We live like gods
Do as we like
Behave as we purpose
Go where we want
Ruin the world and worse
If wishes were all granted
The world would be hell.

Prejudice

Hate is a cross
Some people carry it,
Racism is a cross
Some others bear it,
Religion is a yoke
Around the neck of many
Biased and brainwashed
Initiated and indoctrinated,
Many wear the garment of prejudice.

Innocent, free and fair
Normal and liberal
Just, godly and humane
But prejudice tags him a criminal, terrorist, a rapist.

Fierce anger against a people
Bitter rage on a race
Segregation and discrimination
Class, caste, colour and sexism
Beliefs that are unfair and unjust
Prejudice has done more harm than good.

Lost

Here am I
Lost in myself
Reading this book of mysteries.

Here am I
Lost in the universe
In this diverse nature.

Lost beyond myself
Trying to find a way back
That I may be human again.

But how long will it take
Eternity or shortly,
To be in myself again.

Weird things beyond facts
Crazy people all over
On this bench of loneliness
Invisible yet evincible
Could my words be heard
And my spirit be seen.

The Reading Ghost

See the reading ghost
Beautifully dressed and seated
Reading to learn mysteries.

Look, have you seen an invisible reader
She looks like a tourist
Trying to find out more about others.

Who knows her soul?
Her spirit is unseen,
Who sees her motive?
Her mission is unclear.

This ghost is a teacher
Teaching humans to learn,
Making them wonder.

She is admirable
For this busy world must learn.

When you come across her
Never look for her trouble
For none actually know who she is.

Bandit

The hood is a misery
A total mess
We live by faith alone
To see another day,
Nothing is in order
And life is entirely boring,
We suffer hunger, lack and want
Tomorrow is not just a mystery
But an unpredictable history,
Bandits and vagabonds
Robbers and kidnappers
Killers and assassins
Rapists and womanizers
Drug addicts and alcoholism
We are looking up for hope.

If today is red, how can tomorrow be green?

We die growing up
We grow up dying
We learn suffering
We suffer to learn
Banditry and bigotry
Anarchy and autocracy
Divide and rule
Cruelty and inhumanity
Hardships and warships
And this life makes less sense.

Banditry

The world has gone nuts really nuts
Taboos reign and rule
Abominations dwell and thrive
Sacrileges survive the trend
Atrocities heap like mountains,
No one escapes it all.

The youth is dizzy
Feeling high and intoxicated
Ready to scatter and shatter
Eager to batter and water
Enthusiastic to move on, on that terrific note.

Poisoned, incited and instigated
Polluted, contaminated and infiltrated
Reciting hate, memorizing bitterness
Wanting to push the world off the line
Bandits in banditry
Bandits and banditry
Cooking the world a miserable meal
Paying with their blood
Enlarging the coast of hell.

Cocoon

This is my cocoon
I live here to grow
Just to get ready for the world.

I am in no haste
Time duly pays,
I watch and pray
Hope and wait
Long and yearn
To be free,
Finally free from this cocoon
That I may come show the world
The stuff I am made of.

Wait for me
I am destiny's child
I bring with me blessings
Blessings of profound values
I am coming.

My Shield

Nature is wonderful
See the shield it gave me,
Green, young and strong
Beautiful and exotic
Real, great and nice.

Inside here, I am safe
No more within,
No troubles in here.

I am unstained
Neat, clean and fine
I come out white
For you to knit your wool
Or for your cotton.

I give you clothing
Comfort, warmth and beauty
You look good and exceptional.

I give you money, jobs and connections
I help you build roads and bridges.

I am cotton
The finest piece that fits your body.

Vision

I am an angel
I see beyond the physical
I neither bark nor bite.

Clear and crystal vision
With blue rays of wonder
Seeing and foretelling future.

My whiteness is divine
Reflecting my calmness
My high ears are my horn
Glorious and marvelous.

Of my nose, so unique and outstanding
Of my colours, so naturally adorable,
I am here but I came from afar
I do things beyond the ordinary.

Love me real, and be free
Free from harm and torment
Let me watch and guard you
And keep you safe from evil.

Innocent, peaceful and graceful
Original, symbolic and faithful
Patient, watchful and enduring
I want, I hope, I care.

The purity of my soul
Dwells within and without
The gorgeousness of my being
Explains splendour and valour
I am not like everyday people.

Locomotive

This train is very long
With countless coaches
Moving from the Philippines
Heading for the entire globe,
America, Africa, and Australia
Asia, Europe and the world at large.

Many poets with their pens
Writing to change the world,
A transformation train, dear listeners,
Touching lives, connecting people
Teaching, enlightening
Educating humans, entertaining them
Lifting the downcast and shining light
In a gloomy world of uncertainties.

A locomotive of boundless strength
A fierce engine of measureless might,
Moving in full force
To rid the world of timidity.

Come, join this train
Help fan its engine
This turbine pulls a weighty tale
Let us tell the world a wonderful story.

Heavy Duty

You are a heavy-duty
An earth-moving machine
Find your rail and fix your wheel
Move to your destination.

Young or old, weak or strong
Used and dumped
Or undiscovered
Search for your path and get along.

You are a machine
Full of energy and dreams
There is work to be done
Find it, do it and live it.

You are the powerhouse
The engine of the whole movement,
Fuel yourself and remove the rust
Move, move, move right now.

The road is narrow and slippery
You must find it and keep fit,
If you slip, you crash out
If you derail, you kill dreams
Be on your lane, it is safer that way.

Burn your desire and ignite your passion
Drive your motto and live your watchword,

Forget the smoke, you will not choke
Maintain the scope and raise your hope,
Let your locomotive not rust by the wayside.

Rain, sun, dew, mist
Fog, thunder, lightning,
Autumn, winter, spring
Whichever season, whatever reason
Never be stagnant,
Be a locomotive to the world.

Confusion

I cannot understand
Neither can I comprehend
The actual meaning of politics
If it has to be this fierce.

Why are people killing and being killed?
They mob and get mobbed
Following leaders that are not trustworthy
Heroes that are not conquerors
Legends that are not legendary
And models that are not principled.

I get confused trying to ponder
I get stuck fighting to decipher,
Nothing ever seems understandable.

I mean, why do they keep promising
Knowing fully well that they are lying,
Who are they deceiving when
It has proved severally of their faithlessness.

Politics keeps me troubled and worried
It gives me sleepless nights,
Nights of nightmares and terrors.

I fight with my soul
Trying to conquer the fierceness of the burden,
But the reality dawns on me
That the world is in shambles.

Troubled

The poor is in pain
The gentle is in disarray
The quiet is in danger
The learned is unhappy
The timid is behind
And the rich also cry.

The land is troubled
Everyone in confusion
Helter-skelter, they run
Nothing is in peace
Because we have fooled ourselves.

North, south, east and west
The fire burns, the water rages
Consuming and sinking
Loss, loss, upon the cross.

Yet they think they are safe
They believe they have arrived,
They announce their victory
They celebrate their conquest
Even though they perish.

A people so confused
A generation so bewitched and betrayed
Who shall tell them these horrors?
That they have gone beyond redemption.

The Guardian Dragon

The guardian dragon
Lying still in the park
Watching the children play
As though he is alive.

Green and white
Like a national flag,
With strong horns
And long neck.

Steady, articulate and calm
Ready, committed and dedicated
Focused like a guard
Around free children.

Maybe they like it
Maybe they know it,
Maybe they care not
Maybe they note not
Maybe they are only interested in their game.

The Park

There is a park
There is a dragon
Painted in beautiful colors
It is like a photo.

This park is truly beautiful
Children feel at home,
They play freely and joyously too.

They fear not the dragon
Whether dead or alive,
They have no time for it
Whether a threat or not
They are busy, playing their game
Building their well.

They may be playing with its food
Handling its dish
Concentrated and determined
These two children are beat.

They are not moved
They do what they like
Their day is made
Whoever brought them to this park
Has done them a great thing.

Adventurous children, enthusiastic and curious
Playful couple, conscious of their want
Great duel, partners that learn
Teammates, birds of same feather.

Negligence

Negligence, you are a beast
You have killed humanity
And buried mankind.

Negligence, you are a ghost
You torment society
And haunt our home.

Negligence, you are a skeleton
You haunt our conscience
And taunt our pride.

Negligence, you are a terror
You terrorize our happiness
And enlarge our weakness.

Negligence, you are a shame
You pull our game
And destabilize our peace.

Negligence, you are a sorrow
You shatter our life
And wreak havoc.

Negligence, you are a spirit
Incompetence tells your tale
Imperfection carves your shadow
And troubles leave us to our doom.

Neglected

Down here, we live in tears
Nothing is in shape
Because they care not
But up there, they live in gears
Because they loot the more.

They groove and cruise
While we mourn and suffer
They celebrate and jubilate
While we roast along the coast.

These people are wicked
They have no human sympathy
They are selfish and greedy
Their subjects are in pain.

Deaf ears, they turn to us
Fake promises they make us
False hope they give us
Lies, deceit, hate and division
All they brew to foment troubles.

Divide and rule, tribalism and racism
Religion, war, supremacy and power tussle
They fondle the poor and fumble badly.

Their oath of secrecy
Supersedes their oath of office,

Humans roost, freeze and frozen
Yet they care not.

They have abandoned their duty post
And tortured mankind the most,
They are the evil we fear
It is unfortunate we live with them.

Mr. Bean

Crazy ears
Weird eyes
Rumpled chin
Painted face
Braided hair
Funny head
You look like Mr. Bean.

A comedian
With scary make up
Looking like an alien

Dressed for Halloween
Or ready for Thanksgiving
Going to a movie set
Or to the cinemas.

Some kids would love you
While you might scare others
Life needs some humour
Comedy preferable to tragedy.

Tear the Mask

Life is just once
Let it count,
Do not hide under a ceiling
Let the world receive your best.

Be not a masquerade
Live to the full,
Pretense is a war
It kills many,

Disguise is a cheating
It hinders much,
Fakery is a torment
It blocks blessings.

Tear the mask
Be the real you,
Be proud of yourself,
With yourself and for yourself.

Tear the mask
Never live under a siege
Colours are beautiful
Choose yours wisely
And flaunt them prestigiously.

If you find your scope
Hang in there with hope,

Life is not a joke
So it can choke.

Be the original you
Be not a photocopy,
Teach the world to learn
Let them yearn.

Excellent creation
True creature
Perfect creator
Do not wear a mask.

Hurricane

Hurricane
Wild, weird, whacky
Shuffling, ruffling and rumpling
Killing, scattering and shattering
Confusing, shaking and humiliating
Hurricane, a wind chasing us away.

Beautiful houses defacing
Amazing edifices dismantling
Great erections sinking
Awesome architectural works caving in
Hurricane, a spirit demonizing us.

Creative works rupturing
Pulling down by volcanoes
Like earthquakes and landslides
Sweeping the earth like flood
Vulnerable life we live here.

Colourful artworks dwindling
Wealth going down
Nature succumbing
Beauty fading away.

Hurricane, a force, frictional and destructive
Uncertain, unknown, unleashing.

Conclusion

Yes, I have seen enough
And I need no more evidence
I have understood that life is only for awhile
And we are gone.

We build up treasure and wealth
We bag degrees and credentials
We travel and meet new people
We learn and unlearn many things
We become so rich and famous
That we may never wish to die
But yet we die, sometimes in an undignified way.

We die like a lightning after a terrible thunder
If we manage to thunder aloud,
The noises, shows, glamour and clamour
The wishes, dreams, hopes and aspirations
The achievements and goals
The exposures and experiences
The connections and knowledge
We die and they lie still.

I have concluded that life is a lease
We return it after its expiration
Unfortunately, we are yet to implement this truth.

The truth of the matter is that we live once
Whatever remains when we are gone is legacy

Be it good or bad
Our life and living tells more
As we mark the map, pegging our way
Passersby trace our footprints to follow
to follow our footsteps or not.

Friendship

We are friends
We are one big family
We hold on for each other
And hang out together,
We are many and diverse
From tongues and tribes
We love and care for one another
We are very committed.

Talented, gifted and dedicated
Unique, intelligent, beautiful and pretty
Foresighted, focused and unified
We are one big family.

We kick against hate, racism and tribalism
We fight violence, exploitation and humiliation
We check dehumanization
Our rules are strong and legitimate.

Our friendship is with determination
We decide things together, carrying everyone along
No one has the final say
We discuss and conclude.

Friendship is very necessary
It is a bridge connecting the world
It builds the universe for a better bonding
Nothing can successfully sever a tightened friendship.

Envy, jealousy, anger, evil may raise their ugly heads
But a friendship built on trust and love survives it all.

We Are Friends

Hey, we are friends
Crazy and wonderful
Super and realistic
We live our lives the best we can.

We are friends, hey
Playing and praying together
Reading and studying
Leading and following each other
Teaching and learning from everyone.

Our friendship has come a long way
We have seen the good, the bad and the ugly
Up, down, high, low
We just march on for our sake.

Those who admire us should understand
Those who belittle us should think twice,
Those who stop us should ponder anew
We sacrifice for this union to flourish.

Friends are like families
They neither hurt nor harm themselves
Friends are like soldiers
They protect and secure their territories even with their lives.

Stay away from them
Tear them not apart

But guard and guide them
If there be need
Let them not be limited
For their vision is extraordinary.

The Venom of a Poet

Fear the poet
Play not with his ink
His pen is a beast
And his pen a lion,
His wisdom is magical
And his inspiration divine,
His words are venom.

The venom of a poet
It is inborn
And natural,
Nothing dilutes or neutralizes it
The world fans the flame of his anger.

Happiness, sadness, moodiness, loneliness, weariness, comeliness
Boredom, freedom, stardom
Absurdity, stupidity, ambiguity,
Quietness, silliness, busyness,
Corrections, postulations, assumptions,
Grievances, advances, chances,
Venoms, venomous, voluminous.

Bitterness, the rage of a stage
Calmness, the voice of the dice
Noisiness, the choice of the prize
Venom, the thunder of a poet.

That's my take, take my words
Poisonous, dangerous, ridiculous
We are poets, words choose us

My Ink

My ink is a fire
It burns my flesh
And rekindles my soul,
My ink is a fire
It burns my pain
And ignites my passion.

My ink is a fire
It burns my anger
And enlivens my spirit,
It quenches my thirst
And satisfies my hunger.

My ink is a venom
It hurts, it harms,
It heels, it heals
My ink is a venom
It lives world beyond

My venom, my ink
My spirit, my soul
My feelings, my vision
My ink is a fiery venom.

A venom of kindness
A venom of meekness
A fire of mildness
A fire of gentleness

A venomous fire
Smooth, windy, coolly
Disastrous, dangerous and outrageous
Stay away from its path.

Surrounded

We are soldiers
Fighting for our fatherland
We rest not
We merry neither
We are determined
And dedicated
We put our lives on the line
Our land must be protected
But we are surrounded by the enemy.

No retreat, no surrender
That's what we chant,
No surrender, no retreat
That's all we sing,
Here we are but surrounded.

The enemy is advancing
The enemy is closing in
Here we are, surrounded.

Overrun, outnumbered, surrendered
Captured, defeated, vanquished
O here we are, surrounded.

Hop, hi, hop, hi
Forward march,
Hop, hi, hop, hi
We march to the enemy's camp
In loss, in defeat, in agony
Surrounded, surrendered, defeated.

Delighted in You

Beautiful angel of God
Come, delight my soul
For life I agonize
And living, discouraging.

Holy angel of God
Come, purify my soul
For I need your peace
And total cleansing.

Come, mighty warrior
Come, fight my battles
For they are overwhelming
And breathtaking
Come quick, I need a breakthrough

Come, delight my soul
For I am delighted in you,
Ward off all hateful friends
And ruthless enemies.

Clean messenger of God
Bring me good news
Lift my spirit
And bear my burden
Break every chain
And disentangle all yokes.

Please delight my life
Look away from my lapses
Build me and mould me
Revive me and strengthen me,
Sweet spirit of God
Delight me with your aura,
Let your charisma single me out.

Heaven, delight my heart, body and soul
Quicken these smoldering embers now.

Camouflage

Lost in wonder
Out of misery
It seems like a mystery
For I know not myself,
A part an elephant
Some sides, a butterfly.

Gigantic and large
Huge and intimidating
Brown and chocolate
With horns and folded trunk
I know not my worth.

A caterpillar or cankerworm
Marching in grass or farm
Destroying wheat, corn or millet

I know my size
They have ridiculed me,
Diminished, reduced and abused
Molested, cajoled and belittled
I feel like an ant.

But I look like an elephant
Of course, I am one
Mighty, strong and great
They dare not pull me down.

Scandals

When enemies wake up, they cook
They cook stories that are not true
Because they hate you for reasons or no reasons
They just want to tarnish your image,
The reputation you built ages long.

Rivals carry propagandas
They knit lies carefully well
So that people may believe
And hate you or avoid you

Even friends plant rumours
Colleagues sow discord
Partners work against the band
They gossip, they scandalize
They slander, they dent, they ridicule

Rumours spring from hate, fear, anxiety
Rumours sprout from envy, jealousy, hatred
They aim at cheap blackmail and character assassination.

Rumormongers are mean and heartless
They gain nothing in the end except karma and nemesis,
Because the evil that men do live with them, before
   them and after them.

Falsehood

When they tell you I am a prostitute
Do not listen to them
When they produce evidence
Do not hearken to them
Fear them, these men
They are evil and full of bitterness.

A gang of useless liars
Living lies like life,
A band of merciless accusers
Forging demeaning stories,
They merry from evil
They prove to be evil
They are malicious and dubious.

Fabricated blunders they do
Framed atrocities, they mould
Dirty potters enjoying the craft of pottery
Muddy lunatics murmuring loud
Spitting at angels with boldness.

They run the town and ruin the neighbourhood
False claims, false allegations, false accusations,
Falsehood in the highest order
Their tongues, dark and black
Painting royalty doom.

Treacherous chameleons, cancerous addicts and bandits

Wayward cowards, shameless, possessed and initiated
Always determined to cause havoc

Triggers that kill fame
Cards that play game.

If You See Our Soldiers

If you see our soldiers
Bless them for me
Tell them I am praying for them
That the enemy get subdued.

If you see our soldiers
Let them know we love them,
Tell them they are rare
And their bravery is beyond human.

Tell our soldiers that they are unique
No one can belittle them,
And nothing can ever intimidate them.

If you see our soldiers
Give them a glass of water
Let them quench their thirst,
Shelter them, if they come around
Please show them love
For their strength is unrestricted.

Hug them, and kiss them
Pat them and lift them up,
Give them a high morale
Motivate them and let them fight,
This fight is for a lifetime.

If you see our soldiers
Bless them for me,

Crown them kings
For without them
We are endangered species.

If you see our soldiers
Bless the wombs that bore them
The souls that love them
The arms that cuddle them
And the land they protect.

If you see our soldiers
Give them this piece on my behalf
Tell them I love them all.

Camouflage

You are not the real you
You hide in thick skin
A wolf in sheep's clothing
Pretending to be an angel.

You wear a camouflage, camouflaging
A saboteur, sabotaging
A looter, looting
A thief, stealing
A hunter, hunting
A chameleon, changing
You are a monster
Mustering your unseen arrays
Hitting family and friends
So mean and cruel.

Deceitful, dubious and wayward
Antagonizing, terrorizing
Neutralizing, tormenting
Torturing, haunting and taunting.

Old leopard that never changes
Archaic tortoise, lying, cunning and rude
Weak bat, sitting on the fence.

Masquerade with a heavy mask
Friendly foe beyond the known
You wear a camouflage, camouflaging
You are a saboteur, sabotaging.

My words fail to describe you
Unholy, unruly, untamed
Selfish, greedy, dishonest
The camouflaging chameleon
Tear the mask.

Virgin Santa

Virgin Santa, great with a beautiful heart
Holy, neat and lowly
Gentle, soft, tender and calm
Welcome, welcome dear Santa.

We know you brought us goodness
The news of our saviour's birth
Thank you for the gifts too.

We cherish the presents
They are as beautiful as your heart
We can't wait to have them.

When you go back
Don't forget us
Always come around,
That we may feel loved and refreshed always.

The earth is weary

When Spring Comes In

When spring comes in
Everywhere would be green
Signifying life, fertility, hope and courage.

When spring comes in
The field will be greener, livelier
The farm will be richer, better and softer.

When spring comes in
The moon will be full
The night will be livelier
Tales by moonlight and friendship
Night-outs would be wonderful.

When spring comes in
The vegetation will boom and blossom
Cool and full will be the barns.

Freshness in the air, dew and mist
Showers of rain and blessing
Warmness, announcing fairness.

When spring comes in
The world grows anew, and regenerates.

NGOZI OLIVIA OSUOHA is a Nigerian poet/writer/thinker. A graduate of Estate Management with experience in Banking and Broadcasting.

She has published four poetry books and coauthored one.

She has featured in more than forty international anthologies and also has published over two hundred and fifty poems/articles in over twenty countries.

She has won many international awards and also one time best of the net nominee.

colophon

Poetic Grenade
by Ngozi Olivia Osuoha,
was set with SITKA and HIGHTOWER fonts
by SpiNDec, Treasure Coast, Florida.
The covers were designed
by Kris Haggblom, Port Saint Lucie, Florida.

www.ingramcontent.com/pod-product-compliance
Lightning Source LLC
Chambersburg PA
CBHW030123100526
44591CB00009B/505